THEN & NOW®

AVON

Opposite: This map of southern New England was drawn by students of Avon Old Farms School in 1929. (Historical image courtesy of Avon Old Farms School Archives.)

THEN & NOW®

AVON

Peter J. Wright

Introduction by Nora O. Howard

Dedicated to Carl Candels,
one of Avon's great archivists and community servants.

ISBN 978-0-7385-7381-6

Library of Congress Control Number: 2010927441

Published by Arcadia Publishing
Charleston, South Carolina

Printed in the United States of America

For all general information, please contact Arcadia Publishing:
Telephone 843-853-2070
Fax 843-853-0044
E-mail sales@arcadiapublishing.com
For customer service and orders:
Toll-Free 1-888-313-2665

Visit us on the Internet at www.arcadiapublishing.com

On the Front Cover: Shown is a historic view of Avon Center around 1899 with the New York, Hartford, and New Haven Rail Line heading south to New Haven. Avon Congregational Church continues to stand vigil on the northwest corner at the intersection of Albany Turnpike and Simsbury Road. The contemporary image was taken from the same angle, but now from underneath the branches of Avon's Constitution Pin Oak. (Historical image courtesy of AFPL; contemporary photograph by Peter J. Wright.)

On the Back Cover: This photograph from the 1930s shows how Avon's main intersection was formerly arranged, with the old post office building underneath a far younger Constitution Pin Oak. Before the building on the southeast corner was enlarged, Old Farms Road forked around the oak at Albany Turnpike. (Historical image courtesy of AFPL.)

Contents

Acknowledgments

Many people have helped keep Avon's history alive, passing the torch of collective memory from one generation to the next. Among the prominent torchbearers from our time, Fran Mackie, a gifted storyteller, has set the standard for historical research with her comprehensive work on the history of Avon. Nora Howard, Avon's town historian, a devoted and thorough researcher, conveys a balanced perspective on local history and how it has affected the tenor of Avon.

As for what records remain of our common heritage, Avon Free Public Library (AFPL), in partnership with Avon Historical Society, dedicated the Marian M. Hunter History Room in 1989 to serve as the main repository of Avon's past. Library director Virginia Vocelli manages the collection, assisted by a dedicated core of volunteers who devote their hours to clarifying the archival materials for present and future generations. We owe our gratitude to Jennie Boswell, Carol Dunn, Carol Genco, Ann Mains, and Helen Muszynski. Without their ongoing research efforts, the gathering of collective knowledge about our past would grind to a resounding halt.

We also thank all the private citizens who helped us unravel the past and provided a wealth of information, only a tiny glimpse of which is included in this book. Thanks to Ann August, Charlotte Bennett, Silvio and Terri Brighenti, Steve Brighenti, Janet Carville, Chrissie and John D'Esopo, Irene DeVaux, Marjorie and Carl Dubiel, Dick Holloway and Pam Fahey, Susan Fletcher, Bill Goralski, Nancy and Ray Hanelius, Ines Aramini Hazen, Kathryn Hoidge, Carol Ketcham, Suzanne Macy, Don Malen, Howard Miller, Carolyn "Cal" Miller-Stevens, Victor Mitchell and daughter Carol, J. Anthony O'Neill, Jeannie Parker, Steve Read, Jeanette St. Peter, Jeanette and Albert Simonelli, Ron Simmons, Brad Smith, William Darren Standish, Douglas Thompson, Sandy Trudeau, Aldo Vernesoni, Richard Walker, Lee and Terri Wilson, Fran and Lucienne Witkowski, and Ruth Woodford. We owe our debt of gratitude to these individuals for welcoming us into their lives and helping us with our historical research.

Unless otherwise indicated, contemporary images were photographed by author Peter J. Wright.

INTRODUCTION

The cover photographs on Peter Wright's Then and Now are a condensed history of Avon.

Before there was the Avon Congregational Church Meetinghouse or even a town here, the land was home to the River Indians, a confederation of local tribes who sold the English their land. Farmington was established in 1645, with "Nod" its northern section. In 1750, Nod became a separate parish, known as the "Farmington Second Society," and also as "Northington."

A parish needed its own minister, and Rev. Ebenezer Booge arrived from Yale College in 1751. Northington built its first meetinghouse soon after. Over 50 years later in 1817, a mysterious and maddening fire flattened that little building on a cold December day.

It was a serious situation to be without a meetinghouse, for along with being the spiritual center, people came to the meetinghouse for events and town meetings. The residents were perhaps not entirely surprised at their sudden loss, however. For decades they had been unable to agree on a new site for the successor to their aged meetinghouse. After the fire, they divided the Society and built two different churches: the West Avon Congregational Church (1818) and the Avon Congregational Church (1819).

Transportation routes led south to New Haven and Long Island Sound, west to Albany, New York, north to Northampton, Massachusetts, and east to Hartford and Boston. In 1830, Northington Parish incorporated as the Town of Avon. The Farmington Canal (1828–1847) became Avon's watery highway to the world.

In 1850, railroad tracks followed the failed canal route. These iron horses helped Avon's fuse factory become a major supplier of blasting equipment to shape the U.S. landscape. Immigrants from Italy, Hungary, Poland, Russia, and other countries lived in Avon and worked in the factory, on farms, and on the construction of Avon Old Farms School (1927). The last train charged through Avon in 1991, and today its quiet path is the Farmington Valley Greenway.

Avon has excellent organizations and agencies that preserve local records and sites to share with researchers, as well as the public. Many of the photographs in this book survive due to their diligent efforts to preserve history.

The Avon Free Public Library (www.avonctlibrary.info) operates the Marian M. Hunter History Room, home of an extensive and growing archival collection. In the general library stacks are books and videos on Avon history. The Avon Historical Society (www.avonhistoricalsociety.org) oversees three buildings and the Avon Historical Society oversees three historical properties, maintains proper storage of many artifacts, answers local history questions, offers referrals to those who seek experts to help with their historic home or genealogy questions, and conducts educational programs throughout the year.

The churches have archival collections, and the Avon Town Hall preserves land and probate records from after 1830. Many records previous to 1830 are at the Farmington Town Hall and the Farmington Room at the Farmington Library.

Then and Now author Peter Wright joins other writers and photographers who have recorded, collected, preserved, and celebrated local history. Rev. Rufus Hawley kept a journal for 50 years, from 1763 until 1812. Clinton B. Hadsell took photographs of Avon from 1889 to 1919, when Avon's population was only about 1,000 people. His descendants, Doris Miller and Seth Stewart, donated the Hadsell photographs to the Avon Free Public Library.

Clinton Hadsell's brother Frank wrote down his memories of spending his entire life in Avon, and his thick longhand notebooks cover the years of 1845 to 1942. Lewis S. Mills was a historical writer and photographer, whose work appeared in *The Lure of the Litchfield Hills*, a magazine he edited from the 1940s through the 1960s. Photographers Dwight Douglas and Marvin Deming took hundreds of professional photographs. Among those always willing to share their collections of Avon history and photographs are Gladys August and her late husband, Robert "Bob" August, along with Carl Candels, Janet Carville, John Anthony O'Neill, Jeannie Parker, and Alice Zacchera and her late husband, Ray Zacchera.

Books about Avon include Bill Goralski's stories of Avon in the 1930s–1950s. Marian Thompson and Ruth Thompson complied the gravestone histories of East Avon, West Avon, and Cider Brook Cemeteries (1995). Political memoirs with passages about Avon are Stewart Alsop's *Stay of Execution* (1973) and Joseph W. Alsop's *I've Seen the Best of It* (1992). Elizabeth Winthrop wrote about life on Nod Road in her novel *In My Mother's House* (1988). Mary-Frances MacKie's *Avon, Connecticut, an Historical Story* (1988) is an essential book for the study of Avon. The founder of Avon Old Farms School, Theodate Pope Riddle, is profiled in Sandra Katz's *Dearest of Geniuses* (2003), *A is for Avon* was written by and for local schoolchildren, and finally, my book, *Avon* (2000), has 180 vintage photographs.

For the past two years, Mr. Wright, an architect, photographer, and Avon Historical Society board member, has worked with lenders to identify spectacular historical photographs. These images seem vaguely familiar or utterly beyond recognition and make us laugh, gasp, or sigh at the poignancy of it all. Finding early images of Avon was but half of his job. His modern-day photographs showcase his keen eye and technical skills as a photographer as well as his willingness to stand in the middle of Route 44, tramp through a quiet cemetery, and climb a skinny ladder inside a steeple.

Peter Wright's Then and Now is an eloquent contribution to Avon's history, and a gift to everyone who loves our town.

—Nora O. Howard
Avon Town Historian

CHAPTER 1

AVON CENTER

This is an aerial view of Avon as it appeared in the 1920s, when the Ensign Bickford complex dominated the center of the town and the center's residents timed their clocks to the Ensign Bickford whistle. Today the remaining buildings serve as an office park for town government and several private businesses. (Historical image courtesy of AFPL.)

After numerous cost overruns and delays, the Farmington Canal opened in 1828 and was operational for 20 years. The canal is rightfully credited with helping Avon gain access to broader markets, from Northampton, Massachusetts, in the north to New Haven, Connecticut, in the south. While canal shipments rivaled costs of overland freight, the canal was never a true commercial success, operable only three seasons out of the year and subject to numerous bank breeches during its short commercial life. (Historical image courtesy of AFPL.)

Pictured above is Avon's train depot as it appeared in 1900. Since the Farmington Canal Rail followed along much of the original canal route, a pre-graded section of acquired land, swift implementation allowed for Avon's continued commercial success. Over a century later, sections of the rail line have been replaced by the Farmington Valley Greenway, a unique linear park system, providing considerable pleasure for local residents. (Historical image courtesy of J. Anthony O'Neill.)

Mr. and Mrs. J. P. Neville standing on their farm around 1890, with Avon Congregational Church and O'Neill's Blacksmith Shop in the background to the left. Woodford Avenue meets Simsbury Road in the center. The Avon Creamery Building is in the background to the right. The Nevilles owned a farm that extended north from Sperry Park, south to Avon Post Office, and west to Mountain View Avenue. (Historical image courtesy of AFPL.)

This image from around 1900 shows women and children strolling home from church along Albany Turnpike on a hazy Sunday afternoon. From this vantage point, one can see the Canal Warehouse Building to the left and the old Avon Hotel Building beyond the tree line. New York, New Haven, and Hartford rail line train cars are just visible beyond the warehouse. (Historical image courtesy of C. B. Hadsell Photograph Collection, AFPL.)

Clinton Hadsell captured multiple elements simultaneously when he took this photograph of Avon Center looking north from Avon Old Farms Road around 1900. With train cars stopped near the center of town, Avon Congregational Church's steeple can be seen in the distance left of center, just above the old Avon Hotel. Avon's Constitution Pin Oak—merely a sapling at the time—is just visible to the left of the Canal Warehouse in the far right. (Historical image courtesy of C. B. Hadsell Photograph Collection, AFPL.)

This panorama, taken in 1900 from the steeple of Avon Congregational Church, shows how much has changed in the last century. To the right, one can see the Avon train depot and the Farmington Canal Rail headed north into the distance. The Neville home in the center of the image, now located in Riverdale Farms, is just beyond the long-gone tobacco warehouse. O'Neill's Blacksmith Shop is visible beyond East Avon Cemetery, on the west side of Simsbury Road. (Historical image courtesy of AFPL.)

This image was captured in 1950, following the refurbishing and rededication of the new steeple after it nearly toppled over in the Hurricane of 1938. Originally constructed in 1819, Avon Congregational Church was one of two churches built for a divided congregation following the destruction by fire of the first meetinghouse in 1817. (Historical image courtesy of AFPL.)

Co-Pastor E. Jerome Johanson is seen here preparing for the Easter sermon in 1945, weeks before the end of World War II. Avon Congregational Church's soaring sanctuary has changed little over nearly 200 years of service. (Historical image courtesy of Avon Congregational Church.)

Avon Appliance and Electrical Company, Inc., located in one of Avon's oldest surviving buildings, served as a Baptist meetinghouse at one time. The building stood on Mountain View Avenue from 1818 to 1870 before it was moved to the northeast corner of Albany Turnpike and Simsbury Road, where it served as a succession of shops until 1932. It was moved yet again to its current location on Avon Old Farms Road. (Historical image courtesy of AFPL.)

Erected in 1830, this structure served as the Canal Administration Building for 40 years. It then became the home of Mrs. Cornelius Wheeler from 1872 to 1932. The front half of the ground floor served as Avon's post office from 1946 to 1968, until the postal service moved to its new facility on Enford Street. (Historical image courtesy of Carl Candels.)

Founded in 1917, the Prince Thomas of Savoy Club is a civic and fraternal society organized by the many Italians who came to work at Ensign Bickford and live in Avon. Upon arrival, many Italian immigrants moved into the Old Farms area of town, which led to the construction of the building along Old Farms Road. The historical image shows members gathering for a group portrait, commemorating their 20th anniversary in 1937. The club today welcomes new members and also accommodates the Veterans of Foreign Wars, Post No. 3272. (Historical image courtesy of Carl Candels.)

Hattie and George Read pose with their horse Robert in front of their farmhouse around 1916. It is considered one of the earliest farms in Avon. Evidence of Native American encampment and trading found on the land is now on display at the Peabody Museum in New Haven, Connecticut. The 12-acre farm was later named Towpath, as it backs up to the towpath of the Farmington Canal. (Historical image courtesy of the Read family.)

Frank and Raymond Holloway stand in front of one of their milk trucks around 1950. Frank S. Holloway purchased the Case Farm in 1921, with his brother Ray joining him soon thereafter. Together they rebuilt the dilapidated farm, renaming it Riverdale Farm, and began a dairy herd. By 1932, they started a retail milk business, delivering milk to customers in Hartford. The farm and many of its buildings were converted into a shopping complex by the Brighentis in 1980. (Historical image courtesy of AFPL.)

Avon's train depot, which once stood near where Avon's post office stands today, was in active use from 1850 to 1981. Rather than demolish the old depot, the Brighentis relocated the building to Riverdale Farms and converted it into retail space. (Historical image courtesy of AFPL.)

This image from the Flood of 1955 faces north and shows where Nod Brook severed Simsbury Road. With 14 inches of rain falling mostly through the night over a 36-hour period, residents awoke to find devastation all around them. (Historical image courtesy of J. Anthony O'Neill.)

Sperry Park has served as the backdrop for Avon's love of baseball since 1904, when Franklin M. Sperry provided a section of his cider and sawmill land to be used as a ballpark. When adult teams were popular, the ballpark hosted the "Avon Townies," as in this image from 1912. Formally dedicated in 1934, Sperry Park now has two backstops, scoreboards, a concession stand, and exterior lighting serving Avon's little league throughout the season. (Historical image courtesy of AFPL.)

This image of Towpath School was taken in the 1930s, with additional rooms having been added to the original 1879 schoolhouse at various times. A new brick school was built north of this structure in 1949. The old Towpath School was later converted into a junior high school in 1953 and currently houses the offices of the superintendent and the board of education. (Historical image courtesy of AFPL.)

Towpath School opened in 1949 and was in continuous operation for the next 42 years. Towpath School was opened in response to rapid population growth through the 1930s and 1940s—close to 20 percent per decade. Nationally, education was becoming centralized, and the one-room schoolhouse was going out of fashion. Kindergarten through eighth grade was taught here when Towpath first opened. (Historical image courtesy of AFPL.)

Up until town centers became more urbanized toward the middle of the 19th century, it was common for most families to own a cow or two, or maybe even goats for their own dairy needs. As population centers grew, the need for delivered dairy products became common. Avon Creamery represented that shift in demand. Avon Creamery was a sign of the times, a vertically integrated business, from udder to doorstep, with a full-fledged dairy farm and distribution network. (Historical image courtesy of AFPL.)

The historical image shows the O'Neill men standing in front of their blacksmith shop on Simsbury Road around 1918. It was a transitional moment in time, as America was migrating from horse-drawn transportation to internal combustion. Avon's first gas pump was located on this site. J. Anthony O'Neill's father, John Hayes O'Neill, age 26, is second from the left. B. I. Miller, far right, stands next to his Model T. (Historical image courtesy of J. Anthony O'Neill.)

The view, taken in the 1940s from Avon Congregational Church's steeple, shows how the train line crossed the center of town. The Mobil station, owned by Rene Ruez, occupied the northeast corner while the Avon Grill, Frank Benesio's market, and Primo and Lino Viti's pharmacy occupied the building across the street. The building was later expanded in the direction of the Constitution Pin Oak, narrowing Old Farms Road. Norm's OK Tire Store can be seen in the distance. (Historical image courtesy of AFPL.)

Avon Congregational Church's steeple was rebuilt in the late 1940s, following the Hurricane of 1938. As seen in the photograph from the 1950s, the intersection was confusing at best. When the Farmington Canal Rail ceased operations in 1981, Simsbury and Old Farms Roads were realigned. Traffic lights and raised signage handle today's higher volume of traffic. (Historical image courtesy of AFPL.)

Just east of routes 10 and 44, Mr. and Mrs. Dan Dabica established Avon Colonial Court from six buildings in 1959. Over the next 25 years, neighboring homes, barns, and farm buildings, some dating from the 1830s, were moved, converted, and refurbished to create Old Avon Village, a retail and commercial business district. A 9-foot rocking chair, built by Mr. Bech of Simsbury, was moved there from the Dabica's Elmwood Furniture Company. It continues to serve as Old Avon Village's landmark today. (Historical image courtesy of Old Avon Village.)

Schoolhouse No. 3, otherwise known as "Center School," was built in 1845. It was later named Lewis Mills School in the 1920s. Center School once stood where Avon Free Public Library stands today. It was dismantled, relocated, and reassembled at 8 East Main Street in 1978, where it was restored and converted into Avon's Living Museum. The museum displays artifacts representing 1830, when Avon, formerly Northington, was incorporated. (Historical image courtesy of Sunrise Farm.)

The Avon Water Company was founded in 1911 by local businessmen who were responsible for bringing piped water to the center of town. The first pipeline was dug from Stub Pond to Avon's Center. Most residents still had access to abundant well water. Famous local resident Frank Hadsell found the notion of having running water at the sink far too extravagant and refused to pay for it. (Historical image courtesy of J. Anthony O'Neill.)

Avon's first veterans' honor roll was dedicated with 185 names on May 30, 1943. Avon's Veterans' Memorial now occupies the southwest corner of Avon Green. Memorial Day services are faithfully held here every year. (Historical image courtesy of Carl Candels.)

Fuse manufacturing has been part of Avon's commercial heritage and fame for well over 100 years. The company, established in1852 by Romeo Andrews and Sons, later became known as Climax Fuse, before merging with Ensign Bickford, which continues to operate in Simsbury. This image shows the entrance to the Ensign Bickford Works, when many factory buildings were still constructed of wood in the late 19th century. (Historical image courtesy of AFPL.)

The Avon Volunteer Fire Department was founded in 1943, partly in response to Avon's most famous Canal Warehouse fire in 1936, which nearly razed the center of town. The historical image shows the department's first fire engine, purchased in 1944. Ensign Bickford provided space for the construction of Firehouse No. 1, as seen in the contemporary image. Local fire stations were later established in Secret Lake and West Avon to ensure rapid response to neighborhood fires. (Historical image courtesy of AFPL.)

Stub Pond, along with several other local ponds, was harvested for ice at the turn of the 19th century. Once stored and packed in sawdust, blocks of ice could be kept in a farm's icehouse for up to a year. Ice harvesting, storage, and management played a significant role in Avon's growth and development, with dairy being a critical agricultural product for Farmington Valley. (Historical image courtesy of AFPL.)

Rose's Kitchen opened its doors at 119 Old Farms Road in 1957, offering Italian frozen food to go. Rose Aramini, noted for her meat ravioli and other pasta products such as lasagna, manicotti, meatballs, and sauce, operated the kitchen for 30 years. Her daughter Ines Aramini Hazen took over after Rose passed away in 1987, using the same recipes. Rose's Kitchen moved to Riverton, Connecticut, in 2007, where it is still in operation today. (Historical image courtesy of the Aramini family.)

This vintage postcard from around 1920 shows Adams Campgrounds on the northwest corner of the Albany Turnpike and Route 167. The campground was in operation until World War II, seemingly on the edge of civilization at that time. In the backwoods, the Hartford Gun Club shot skeet. (Historical image courtesy of Carl Candels.)

CHAPTER 2

Nod

Nod is Avon's first commercial focal point. There has been a stopping point or way station, whether an inn or tavern, at the juncture of Nod and Waterville Roads and the Albany Turnpike for over 300 years. It also marks the eastern edge of Farmington Valley. (Historical image courtesy of AFPL.)

Gilbert F. Heublein, a celebrated German-born hotelier, restaurateur, and gourmet food and liquor innovator from Hartford, Connecticut, built the tower in 1914 as a summer retreat for his family and to entertain weekend guests. This historic aerial view of the tower and grounds dates from around 1920. (Historical image courtesy of Heublein Tower Archives.)

Heublein Tower has enjoyed its share of famous visitors. This vintage photograph, taken in the 1950s, shows Ronald Reagan, then president of the Screen Actors Guild, attending a barbecue hosted by the *Hartford Times*. President Reagan is seen here posing with dining hall staff. (Historical image courtesy of Heublein Tower Archives.)

This image, taken on March 26, 1911, shows a large group of people posing for the camera in front of Avon's Split Rock, a unique rock formation left here by receding glaciers on top of the Talcott Mountain Range. (Historical image courtesy of AFPL.)

This is one of several photographs taken by Clinton B. Hadsell as Avon Mountain Road was being regraded and widened in 1911. Avon Mountain Road's design has been under review for several generations. (Historical image courtesy of C. B. Hadsell Photograph Collection, AFPL.)

In 1895, only a tiny fraction of Connecticut's 12,000 miles of roadway were paved. James Henry MacDonald, Connecticut's first traffic commissioner, led a movement to begin paving many of the state's overland routes. Avon and Farmington Valley's growth would have been severely hampered in the early 20th century had it not been for the full development of Avon Mountain Road and the Albany Turnpike. The MacDonald Memorial, overlooking Farmington Valley from the side of Avon Mountain Road, was dedicated August 30, 1933. (Historical image courtesy of AFPL.)

Joseph North's Blacksmith Shop, built in 1832 near the northeast corner of Nod Road and Albany Turnpike, is visible on the far right of the contemporary image. A large section of land was granted to John North in 1678, "under the mountain and north of the Hartford-Albany Turnpike," by King Charles II, in gratitude for his service during King Phillip's War. Avon Old Farms Inn began in 1923, when existing buildings were connected to create the inn seen today. (Historical image courtesy of AFPL.)

The original 24-unit Avon Old Farms Motel was built on this southeast corner of the Albany Turnpike and Waterville Road in 1955. After two expansions, it has grown into a 160-room luxury hotel. Today the Avon Old Farms Hotel is part of the Classic Hotels of Connecticut Collection run by the Brighenti family, which includes the Farmington Inn, The Simsbury 1820 House, and The Simsbury Inn. (Historical image courtesy of Carl Candels.)

The Woodford Farm is Connecticut's 10th oldest family farm, being continuously run by members of the Woodford family since 1666. The Pickin' Patch, where customers come to pick their own pumpkins, vegetables, and a variety of berries, was born after a freak winter storm ruined that year's tobacco crop in 1977. Donald Carville planted $30 worth of pumpkin seed over 4 acres of devastated tobacco fields. From that initial $30 investment, the Carvilles sold $3,000 worth of pumpkins that fall. (Historical image courtesy of Janet Carville.)

This image from the Flood of 1955 shows the perspective from Mountain View Avenue looking east down Albany Turnpike. The Esso Station and Avon Diner in the distance were washed down the turnpike, ultimately landing where Blue Fox Golf Course is today. The rain and flooding advanced rapidly overnight. Much of the floodwater drained into the Long Island Sound two days later, leaving devastation throughout the state. (Historical image courtesy of AFPL.)

CHAPTER 3

West Avon

West Avon has long been known for farming. This southeastern aerial view from the early 1950s speaks to Avon's agricultural heritage. Julius Rottenberg's nursery, Northern Landscape Tree Farm, on the corner of West Avon Road and Sunrise Drive, occupies the upper left of the image. Sunrise Farm's cupola and silos are visible in the center. The farm was a diversified commercial operation, producing dairy products, poultry, potatoes, outdoor tobacco, field corn, and hay. (Historical image courtesy of Sunrise Farm.)

Chartered in 1788, the 1st Company Governor's Horse Guard was composed of prominent Hartford men, many of them veterans of the War of Independence. They served as mounted honor guards for the governor and as ceremonial escorts to prominent visitors. The historical image shows 1st Company on parade in 1888. The honor guard has been stationed in Avon since 1954, and members continue to uphold its traditions. The unit welcomes visitors and actively trains new volunteers. (Historical image courtesy of 1st Company Governor's Horse Guard Archives.)

Thanks to a donation of land by the Manion family, St. Ann's Church was dedicated in 1919 on Mountain View Avenue. The church, shown in this historic view from the 1940s, seated 150 parishioners. St. Ann's moved to its current location on West Avon Road in 1957 and now serves over 2,000 families. (Historical image courtesy of AFPL.)

This farmhouse was one of three Derrin family homes built along West Avon Road. Originally built around 1810, the home was occupied by Derrins and their descendants up until 1954, when the Governor's Horse Guard acquired the property for use as a caretaker's cottage. Avon Historical Society began restoration in 1996. It now serves as one of the society's interpretive museums, modeled as a turn-of-the-19th-century farmhouse, locally known as the "Derrin House." (Historical image courtesy of AFPL.)

In the 1940s, just as Miller Foods, Inc., was getting started by Henry Miller, this photograph was taken of the original Miller barn. Cal and Sandy have continued the family business for more than 60 years, with the fourth generation of Millers now actively involved in growing the business. (Historical image courtesy of Miller Foods, Inc.)

A member of the D'Esopo family took this photograph just as they embarked on the restoration of this nearly forgotten Derrin home in 1985. The home was originally built around 1810 by Derrin family descendants. Every summer, Chrissie D'Esopo hosts a garden tour to raise funds for various non-profit causes in the greater Hartford area. (Historical image courtesy of the D'Esopo family.)

The tradition of libraries in Avon goes back to 1791, when Rev. Rufus Hawley collected money to buy books for the first library. Over the next century, the library was located in a harness shop, retail store, and private homes until August 30,1932, when the first structure, built expressly for the library, was dedicated. Avon Free Public Library's size and mission have expanded greatly since those humble beginnings, now sited on Country Club Road. (Historical image courtesy of AFPL; contemporary image, courtesy of Tad Kuziak.)

West Avon Congregational Church was built in1818 to replace the dilapidated 66-year old edifice known as the Church of Christ in Northington, which was destroyed by fire in 1817. Siting of the new church was a divisive issue. The worshippers originally built West Avon Congregational in the geographical center of town to replace the old meetinghouse, while Avon Congregational was erected a year later in the town's commercial center. West Avon Church's members include local families whose roots go back to the church's earliest development, who have been ministering to communities far and wide for over 260 years. (Historical image courtesy of C. B. Hadsell Photo Collection, AFPL.)

Rev. Ronald Kurtz is seen here in front of the choir in the early 1960s. The decorative organ pipes seen in the background are on display in the Victorian bridal room. From 1869 to 1965, West Avon Congregational Church sanctuary occupied the upper floor, until the congregation moved and restored the double-height sanctuary in 1969. The cross mounted on the north wall of the sanctuary is made of hand-hewn chestnut beams from the original 1818 structure. (Historical image courtesy of West Avon Congregational Church Archives.)

Sunnybrook Ice Cream Bar was owned and operated by George and Irene De Vaux. Jean and Bob Gaudette are seen posing in front of the establishment in 1951. The expansive farmland beyond, to the right of the ice cream bar, is where Avon High School stands today. (Historical image courtesy of AFPL.)

The Golf Club of Avon began in 1925, when Samuel Graham purchased the 60-acre Stilwell Farm with the intent of developing it into a golf course. The club has since expanded from 9 to 27 holes, allowing players considerable versatility with three separate 18-hole courses. Since 1980, there have been ongoing renovations and additions. Tennis and paddle courts as well as swimming pools have been added to accommodate year-round membership. (Historical image courtesy of the Golf Club of Avon Archives.)

In 1936, a local physician knew that Gertrude Petersen was a gifted caretaker for ill family members. He asked if she would care for an elderly patient who was to be discharged from the hospital without family to take her in. Gertrude and her husband, Nick Petersen, agreed. Thus began the West Avon Convalescent Home in the Petersen farmhouse. Soon other doctors sent more patients. This first nursing home in Farmington Valley evolved into the present-day Avon Health Center. (Historical image courtesy of Jeanette St. Peter.)

Valley Community Baptist Church began in 1976 when a small group began discussing the need to start an evangelical church in the Farmington Valley. Within a few months, the group commenced services at Avon Middle School and called their first pastor, Ken Peterson. In 1980, ground was broken in Avon. A new sanctuary, education wing, and fellowship hall were added in the 1990s, along with a new classroom building in 2003. Valley Community Baptist Church welcomes over 1,700 worshippers each weekend. (Historical image courtesy of Valley Community Baptist Church.)

This home, built in 1840, was once occupied by E. M. Woodford, a well-known surveyor of the time. The photograph, taken in 1978 by Avon Historical Society's Home Survey Project, provides a glimpse of how rural West Avon was up until the 1980s, before suburban development started to fill in West Avon and Huckleberry Hill Roads. (Historical image courtesy of AFPL.)

The Avon Festival of October 15, 1975, was an early bicentennial celebration held in the field in front of Sycamore Hills Park. The event honored 60 longtime dedicated community volunteers, with special honors for Dr. William Wiepert and Oliver Thompson. Seated below are, from left to right, Oliver and Betty Thompson and Dr. Wiepert with his wife, Louise. The site later became the home of Avon Senior Center. (Historical image courtesy of AFPL.)

Robert J. Holmes, Civil War vet and former prisoner of Andersonville, is seen here in this photograph from 1920. He was then retired from his varied careers involving politics, agricultural endeavors, and sawmill and gristmill operations in the Sleepy Hollow area. This home is one of a remaining handful of historic homes that line the southern reaches of West Avon Road. (Historical image courtesy of Sunrise Farm.)

Several generations of the Burnham family are seen here posing for the camera while loading hay for the barn in the 1920s. The field behind the tree to the right is the location of Avon High School today. The Burnhams donated a northern section of acreage in the 1920s for the creation of the West Avon Community Club, West Avon's social center, providing local entertainment and activities through dances, barbecues, water carnivals, holiday parties, and talent shows for nearly 75 years. (Historical image courtesy of the Burnham family.)

In this photograph, father Joe Thompson is in the driver's seat with mother Susan and children Reata and Oliver in back, off for a drive in their 1916 Overland. The Thompson family has been involved in agriculture in Avon for seven generations. The Sunrise Farm remains active, having raised pigs, horses, Holstein cattle, and numerous crops for over 150 years. (Historical image courtesy of Sunrise Farm.)

District No. 7 Schoolhouse, locally named Pine Grove School, now serves as Avon Historical Society's Schoolhouse Museum, interpreted as a turn-of-the-19th-century schoolhouse with authentic classroom desks and textbooks from the era. The school was in operation from 1865 to 1949, built at a cost of $1,538.34, and considered a highly innovative design for its time. (Historical image courtesy of AFPL.)

The image of Pine Grove School's interior from 1912 helped Avon Historical Society recreate the school's current interpretation. Teachers were typically single women who boarded in local homes and were usually employed for one or two years before moving on to marry and raise families. Class sizes varied from 8 to 30 students from year to year, serving grades one through eight. Former students have fond memories of their one-room schoolhouse and continue to serve as museum interpreters. (Historical image courtesy of AFPL.)

Originally organized in 1845 by residents of Unionville who desired an alternative to worshipping at the Congregational meetinghouse, Christ Episcopal Church is recognized as one of the first Episcopal churches in Farmington Valley. Services were held in parishioners' homes until a church was completed in 1871 in Unionville. Road widening brought the congregation to Avon in 1965. Parishioners come from all over the valley to participate in the life and worship of the parish. (Historical image courtesy of Christ Episcopal Church.)

Leon and Bertha "Maude" Smith purchased over 120 acres in 1922, then known as Pine Grove Farm. In the 1930s, Leon delivered milk and cream daily to Hartford's Heublein Hotel. Son Max grew apples and peaches, and folks began calling the farm "Smith's." Smith Farm of Avon is still a thriving fruit orchard, also selling homegrown rhubarb, berries, and vegetables. (Historical image courtesy of Lucienne Witkowski.)

The first Memorial United Methodist Church was built in Unionville in 1867. Following urban renewal in Unionville during the late 1960s, Memorial United moved to its present site where the cornerstone was dedicated in 1970. In 1972, the Churchery Nursery School was opened. In 1992, a new education wing was dedicated. In 2006, the old cornerstone from the Unionville Church was reconditioned and is on display. Several stained glass windows from the old church are now on exhibit in the main sanctuary. (Historical image courtesy of Memorial United Methodist Church.)

Ray Hanelius, a teacher and scientist, fulfilled his dream of "working the land" by developing Applegate Farms in 1979. Purchasing land on Huckleberry Hill, he planned and established a family-owned and -run fruit farm. In 2000, he sold a portion of the farm, selling building lots with apple, peach, and nectarine trees. Later, he mentored the new owners, to help them realize an annual crop of fruit for their families. (Historical image courtesy of the Hanelius family.)

This original parcel of land was deeded by King George III to James Woodford in 1773. The home that stands there today was built by Woodford in 1779. The image shows Susie and Clarence Hutchins with their horse in front of the farmhouse around 1920. During the Great Depression, Oliver Thompson said, "The West Avon area was 'like one big family' and where there was need, someone was there to offer assistance." (Historical image courtesy of Richard Hutchins Walker.)

Countryside Park was built in 1968. It was developed from a parcel of land acquired from the Unionville Water Company as demand for taxpayer-supported recreation areas arose. It was described as "a monument to community effort and cooperation" by the building committee. For Avon, with its deep agricultural roots, Countryside Park marked the beginnings of the town's evolution into suburbia. (Historical image courtesy of AFPL.)

Victoria and Anna Bekalik pose in front of one of the last remaining bank barns in Avon around 1920. The barn served as the main cow barn for a 400-acre dairy farm that stretched along both sides of Huckleberry Hill Road. The Bekaliks bought and worked this farm from 1911 through the 1920s. Their son George, an avid farmer and mechanically gifted innovator, continued to operate the farm through the 1960s. (Historical image courtesy of Marjorie and Carl Dubiel.)

This home was built in 1811 by Romanta Woodruff and Hannah Robbins. Woodruff was a farmer, distiller, and exporter of apples, cider, and butternuts to the West Indies. In 1844, the widowed Hannah Woodruff sold the house and acreage to her son Daniel for "$300 plus board and clothing as long as she shall live." In 1897, the house was passed on to Carrie Woodruff and her husband, Milton H. Edwards, the Avon selectman for whom Edwards Road is named. (Historical image courtesy of AFPL.)

Cherry Park was once one of Connecticut's main fairgrounds featuring 4H fairs and sulky racing around the turn of the 19th century, reportedly attracting visitors from over 50 miles away. Cherry Park later operated midget auto and stock car races, as well as demolition derbies during the 1950s. Residents on the other end of town recall hearing the drum of revving engines on weekend evenings. The area was converted into single-family homes in the 1980s. (Historical image courtesy of AFPL.)

Some of Secret Lake's residents are seen here taking advantage of a warm summer evening in the 1930s. Once known as Cherry Pond, developers renamed it Secret Lake in 1928, selling summer cottages and campsites along the lake's edge. The Secret Lake Association was incorporated in 1931. Many cottages that lined the lake were converted into single-family homes after World War II, and residents continue to enjoy lake activities all year round. (Historical image courtesy of AFPL.)

St. Matthew Lutheran Church began in 1885 in Collinsville. It was originally organized as the German Evangelical Lutheran Church of St. Matthew, a community of faith for the German immigrants who settled here. Reorganization of Collinsville following the Flood of 1955 brought the congregation to Avon. The sanctuary was dedicated in 1963, with education and fellowship wings added in 1970 and 2006. Today the church serves a large and diverse congregation, welcoming all who come to worship. (Historical image courtesy of St. Matthew Lutheran Church.)

Lovelytown School was in continuous operation as a one-room schoolhouse from 1831 to 1949. Louise Lusk wrote about the school in 1949, commenting that teachers "taught faithfully and well midst great handicaps . . . children could write, spell and figure . . . better than they can today and the ungraded school of the past had nothing to be ashamed of unless it was the low wages the teacher received." (Historical image courtesy of AFPL.)

CHAPTER 4

CIDER BROOK

The Cider Brook area is where Avon began. The first homesteads were built in this location, as settlers began to develop land north of Farmington along the east side of Farmington River. Home to the area's first meetinghouse, Cider Brook Cemetery is also where many of Avon's founding families and their descendants lie buried. (Historical image courtesy of the author.)

Janice Loeffler's contemporary painting depicts the conflagration of the "Lord's Barn," Northington's first meetinghouse, in 1817. Built in 1750 by Northington's growing population in the northern section of Cider Brook, the meetinghouse burned down 67 years later in a suspicious fire. Having located the site of the first meetinghouse over 200 years later, the men in the photograph are, from left to right, Clarence B. Curtis, Austin Hunter, Edward Prowe, and C. F. Woodford. They stand behind a marker stone dedicated in 1958. (Historical image courtesy of J. Anthony O'Neill.)

Taken in the1920s in the Sleepy Hollow area of West Avon, this photograph shows the purported birthplace of Wilford Woodruff, fourth president of the Church of Jesus Christ of Latter-day Saints. The farm of about 40 acres also included a sawmill and gristmill. (Historical image courtesy of Sunrise Farm.)

Cyclists are seen here at the turn of the 19th century, enjoying a day out in a wooded, hilly section of West Avon known as "Sleepy Hollow." The cyclists are, from left to right, Walter Judd, unidentified, Martha "Mattie" Holmes, Ethel Colvin, Robert J. Holmes Jr., and Amy Colvin. The 12 homes, a gristmill, and a sawmill in this area were sold to Theodate Pope Riddle to build Avon Old Farms School for Boys. The buildings were demolished, and the area reverted to woodland. (Historical image courtesy of Sunrise Farm.)

Avon Old Farms School was conceived and founded by visionary female architect and developer Theodate Pope Riddle. Mrs. Riddle designed all the original buildings of this remarkable campus, basing her designs on visits to the English Cotswalds, using local timber, stone, and slate. Avon Old Farms, which started with only a small student population in its first year, has now grown to a 400-student population from all over the world. (Historical image courtesy of Avon Old Farms School Archives.)

Longtime friend of President Franklin and First Lady Elizabeth Roosevelt, Theodate Pope Riddle, leased Avon Old Farms School to the government as a rehabilitation base for partially and fully blinded servicemen from 1944 to 1948, naming it Old Farms Convalescent Hospital. Over 800 trainees were conducted through a four-month program with courses in braille, musical instruments, typing, woodworking, machinery, automobile mechanics, as well as skills for daily living. (Historical image courtesy of AFPL Photograph Collection.)

Only four months before the great Flood of 1955, Stanley Fisher bought 900 acres east of Avon Old Farms School to develop factory sites. In the hours following the flood, Fisher speculated on what could be done with the devastated property. Stanley Fisher began quarrying from a rich gravel bed out of the northeast section, where Spring Lake is today. Stanley Fisher later donated 279 acres of this land to the town of Avon, today known as Fisher Meadows, in his honor. (Historical image courtesy of Avon Department of Parks and Recreation Archives.)

This 900-acre, low-lying section of farmland that stretches from Simmons Family Farm on Avon's southeastern edge to Fisher Meadows in the north was once part of Avon Old Farms School Property. A pair of Avon Old Farms blue ribbon horses is seen on Tillitson Road in the 1930s. (Historical image courtesy of Avon Old Farms School Archives.)

The Simmons family has been operating this 450-acre, 60-cow dairy farm for over a decade. The farm was originally used for Avon Old Farms School's agricultural program for over 25 years, sited between Old Farms Road and the Farmington River on Tillitson Road. The Flood of 1955 washed away the farmhouse shown in the historical image. The surviving barn's upper window sills in the background indicate how high the floodwaters reached. The horse barn on the left side of the contemporary image was rebuilt in 1999. (Historical image courtesy of Simmons Family Farm.)

The Farmington Canal Aqueduct was a distinctive landmark in Cider Brook. For an early-19th-century generation that rarely experienced the world from great heights, some described the view from 40 feet above the surface of Farmington River as "breathtaking." The stone pillars survived in ruins for over a century. Following the Flood of 1955, the Department of Environmental Protection removed all but the still-visible bank pillars, determining them to be an impediment to flood control. (Historical image courtesy of AFPL.)

Not only was this area well-known for the aqueduct and later "pillar ruins" for over 100 years, but this shallow and slow section of the Farmington River is still recognized as a popular recreational spot, accessible from a unique towpath park near Cider Brook's southeastern edge. (Historical image courtesy of C. B. Hadsell Photograph Collection, AFPL.)

Consistent with our mission to preserve history on a local level, this book was printed in South Carolina on American-made paper and manufactured entirely in the United States. Products carrying the accredited Forest Stewardship Council (FSC) label are printed on 100 percent FSC-certified paper.